The Nature Adventure Book

Written by **Katie Taylor**
Illustrated by **Lianne Harrison**

Contents

Look out for this symbol. It means there are some hints and tips about mindfulness.

Adventure skills

Let's go on an adventure together! Can you find me hiding throughout this book?

Nature detective

DK | Penguin Random House

Author Katie Taylor
Illustrator Lianne Harrison
Editor Sally Beets
Project Art Editor Vic Palastanga
Consultant Derek Harvey
US Senior Editor Shannon Beatty
Additional Design Polly Appleton
Managing Editor Penny Smith
Managing Art Editor Mabel Chan
Production Editor Abi Maxwell
Senior Production Controller Ena Matagic
Creative Director Helen Senior
Publishing Director Sarah Larter

First American Edition, 2021
Published in the United States by DK Publishing
1450 Broadway, Suite 801, New York, NY 10018
Copyright © 2021 Dorling Kindersley Limited
DK, a Division of Penguin Random House LLC
21 22 23 24 25 26 10 9 8 7 6 5 4 3 2 1
Copyright © 2020 Dorling Kindersley Limited
A Penguin Random House Company
10 9 8 7 6 5 4 3 2 1
001–321631–March/2021

Published in Great Britain by Dorling Kindersley Limited.
A catalog record for this book is available from the Library of Congress.
ISBN: 978-0-7440-2666-5

Wild art

Sensory games

Make sure that your child only collects flowers or leaves that have fallen on the ground and avoids picking up anything that is poisinous.

This symbol shows where there is safety information for parents.

⚠️

Safety information

Outdoor recreational activities are by their very nature potentially hazardous. All participants in such activities must assume the responsibility for their own actions and safety. If you have any health problems or medical conditions, consult with your physician before undertaking any outdoor activities. The information contained in this guide book cannot replace sound judgment and good decision making, which can help reduce risk exposure, nor does the scope of this book allow for disclosure of all the potential hazards and risks involved in such activities. Learn as much as possible about the outdoor recreational activities in which you participate, prepare for the unexpected, and be cautious. The reward will be a safer and more enjoyable experience.

Printed and bound in China

This book was made with Forest Stewardship Council ™ certified paper—one small step in DK's commitment to a sustainable future. For more information go to www.dk.com/our-green-pledge

FSC
www.fsc.org
MIX
Paper from responsible sources
FSC™ C018179

For the curious
www.dk.com

Journey stick

A journey stick is a memento of your outdoor adventures. Make one by collecting things like flowers and leaves, and tying them to a stick. Then you can use your special stick to tell people the tales of your adventures.

You will need:
- natural items found on the ground
- string or sticky tape
- long stick

1 Every time you go out on a journey, pick up a natural object to remind you of your trip. It could be the shell you used to decorate a sandcastle, or a leaf from a tree you climbed.

2 Use string or sticky tape to attach your treasure to a stick.

My stick may be small, but I've been on BIG adventures.

Space out your mementos along the stick.

Adventure skills

4

You can add shells, feathers, stones, or whatever you want to your stick.

Use your journey stick to share the **stories of your adventures**, explaining the secrets behind each item you've kept. The Indigenous Peoples of North America and Australia have used sticks in similar ways for many years.

What does each object remind you of?

The longer the stick, the more treasures you can tie to it!

⚠️

Be mindful of what your child collects. Make sure they only choose things that are loose on the ground.

Finding your way

Explorers carry compasses to help them navigate when out in the wild. Did you know that you can make one using just a leaf, a pin, and a magnet?

Adventure skills

⚠️

Supervise your child when holding the needle.

1 Rub a magnet along the length of a needle around 50 times. Lift it off after each stroke.

2 Lay the needle on the center of a leaf.

3 Carefully place the leaf in a bowl of water. The leaf will begin to move slowly before it settles into a North/South position.

4 Now you need to figure out which end is North. Poke a stick into the ground and mark where the end of the shadow lies on the ground using a pebble. After 30 minutes, mark where the shadow has moved to.

If you stand between the two marked points, with the first on your left and the second on your right, you will be facing North.

N

S

North

Once you know
which end of the
needle is North,
you can place
stones in North,
East, South, and
West positions.

West

East

You can also place the leaf on a puddle of water, as long as it's not windy!

Use your compass
to play a **treasure hunt**
game with a friend.
First, hide some "treasure"
(this could be a special toy),
then direct your friend using
North, East, South, and
West clues.

South

I've found
the treasure!

Secret shelters

Get all your friends involved in the fun of building an outdoor den together. It will make the perfect secret hideout.

You will need:
- long branches
- sturdy tree
- smaller sticks
- fallen leaves
- logs
- fallen flowers

Adventure skills

1 Place your first two branches against your chosen tree, ensuring that they are stable.

2 Arrange the rest of the branches against the first two. Aim to make a cone shape.

3 Fill in any gaps with smaller sticks and leaves, weaving in and out of the frame you have built.

You can decorate your shelter with fallen flowers and leaves.

4 Roll logs into your shelter for seating.

Help your child to secure the branches safely against the tree.

Tiny den
You can also build a special small shelter for little creatures. Make it extra comfy by laying out a bed of leaves on the ground.

That looks cozy!

9

Nifty knots and wonderful weaves

Learning to tie knots is a really handy life skill. Once you've got the knack of the knots at the bottom of the page, use your new talent to create a wonderul nature weave.

1 Follow the instructions in the panel below to tie the sticks together to create a frame.

2 Loop string around the top and bottom sticks. Space out each loop as shown.

Knots

Follow these steps to secure your sticks. Start with a clove hitch, then tie a square lashing. Tying knots can be a bit tricky, but it's excellent exercise for your fingers!

Clove hitch

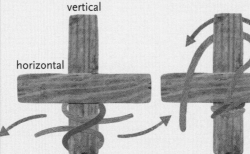

vertical

horizontal

1 Start by tying the string as shown, underneath where the sticks cross.

Square lashing

2 Loop the string around the back of the vertical stick and over the horizontal stick.

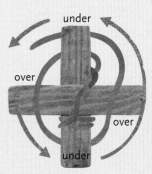

under

over

over

under

3 Continue to loop the string over and under, all the way around.

Immerse yourself in the **slow and mindful** process of weaving. Weaving in and out can help us to connect with nature and find calm.

3 Now you can get creative! Weave the natural items in and out of the string.

Can I hang that weave up in my burrow?

You could also use a Y-shaped branch instead of creating a frame.

4 Repeat the previous action three times, then pull the string tight.

5 Loop the end of the string underneath the stick as shown.

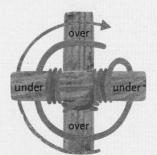

over

under   under

over

6 Pull the string over, under, then over the sticks again.

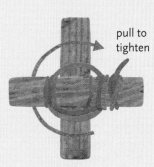

pull to tighten

7 Thread the end of the string under the last loop and tighten to finish.

11

Terrific twig raft

Building a twig raft provides hours of fun. You can put it to the test by sailing it on a river, the ocean, your local pond, or in a water tray at home!

You will need:
- seven sticks
- string
- leaf

Adventure skills

1 Gather six sticks of roughly the same length and thickness for the base, and one thinner stick for the mast.

2 Lay out your base sticks and, at one end, weave the string around each stick in turn before securing it with a knot. Repeat at the other end.

3 Poke your mast stick through the middle of the base. Tie it in place by looping string around the mast twig and then under the raft.

mast

4 Poke the mast through a leaf to make the sail.

Try using different leaves for the sail. Which one makes the raft travel fastest?

This simple activity combines **art**, **science**, **math**, and **engineering**!

⚠️

Rivers, ponds, and the ocean can be dangerous. Always accompany your child when near the water's edge.

Nature hunt

You will need:
- pen or pencil
- paper

The natural world is a treasure trove of things to discover. Go on a hunt to find out what you can spot. Make a list of things you'd like to see, or take inspiration from these lists, then check the items off when you find them.

Nature detective

While on your nature hunt, pay close attention to the way that things around you look and feel. What describing words would you use for them?

Find things that are...

- ☐ colorful
- ☐ shiny
- ☐ smooth
- ☐ rough
- ☐ pointy
- ☐ soft
- ☐ pretty
- ☐ prickly

Try sketching some of the interesting things you find.

I bet you can't find me!

I spy a...

☐ spiderweb

☐ tree

☐ butterfly

☐ cloud

☐ flower

☐ ant

☐ feather

☐ stick

☐ rock

☐ bird

☐ pine cone

☐ set of paw prints

15

Bug hotel

Welcome tiny creatures into your garden by building them a cozy place to stay.

Nature detective

1 Carefully stack wooden crates on top of each other. Make sure you do this on flat, stable ground.

2 Fill the gaps between your crates with different materials. Create smaller spaces by slotting in bricks, logs, and plant pots.

Fill spaces with grass and fallen leaves.

Can I stay here too?

Bug hotels are a great way to recycle garden waste.

Spotting creatures

From under the ground to on top of colorful flowers, bugs can be found in all kinds of outdoor spaces.

Bright flowers attract butterflies.

Caterpillars crawl on fresh leaves.

You find dragonflies by ponds.

Once you have created your **bug home**, keep checking for new visitors. Study your new friends and note down what you observe.

Bricks make perfect insect hiding places.

Bees burrow inside bamboo.

Bugs like to hide underneath big logs.

Damp soil is ideal for worms.

Smart spiders wait on their webs to trap bugs to eat.

Groups of ants live inside little hills.

Whatever the weather

There's an old saying that there's "no such thing as bad weather, just bad clothing." There's a fun activity here for every type of weather. What will you try first?

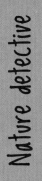

Rain

Rain is tiny droplets of water falling from clouds. Experiment next time it's raining by putting containers out and guessing which will fill up first!

Take some pots and pans outside and let the rain **make music**.

Dip your hands into **muddy puddles** and print them onto tree trunks or the sidewalk.

Search for rainbows! The best time to find them when it is sunny and rain.

When water freezes, it turns to ice.

Add salt and food coloring to a block of ice and watch amazing **patterns** appear.

Snow

When it's very cold, snow falls from clouds instead of rain. It's so much fun to play in, but remember to wrap up warm!

Make **ice art**! Place plants that you find on the floor and the ends of a piece of string into a jar lid, then fill it up with water. Put it in the freezer. When it's frozen, you'll have a pretty decoration to hang outside!

Lie down and move your arms and legs to make snow angels.

Put different objects on a tray and see whether they melt in the sun.

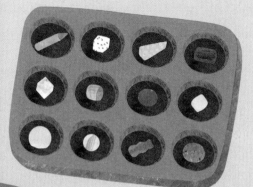

Sun

Warm, sunny days are great for all kinds of outdoor activities—like **making a sundial**! Poke a paper straw through a paper plate and watch as the shadow moves around the plate throughout the day. This is because the Earth rotates around the sun, which makes the sun's position in the sky appear to move.

Go outside and get a friend to **draw around your shadow using chalk**. Then do it again later in the day. Is the shadow in the same place?

When out in the sun, remember to wear a hat, put on sunscreen, and drink water!

Wind

When air moves from one place to another, this is called wind. Make a **wind catcher** by threading strands of ribbon onto a hoop. Hold it up in the air—can you tell which way the wind is blowing?

A simple **game** for a windy day is to lay out different sized objects, like rocks, feathers, and toys, and guess which will blow the farthest.

Tie a white sheet around two trees, with the bottom of the sheet resting on the floor. See what blows into it! Don't forget to take it down when you've finished.

Whoosh!

19

Sky gazing

The sky is always changing—it looks different every day. Look up... what can you see today?

Make a **cloud spotter**. Cut a rectangle from the middle of some oaktag, decorate it, then attach a stick for the handle. Peek through the hole. Can you see any of the cloud shapes listed below?

Nature detective

Cloud watching

Clouds are made up of tiny droplets of water or ice that float in the sky. There are many different types to spot—some tower high up while others linger close to the ground.

Cirrus clouds are wispy streaks of white formed high up in the sky.

Altocumulus clouds look like woolly sheep. They appear in clumps called "cloudlets."

Cumulus clouds are white and puffy. They can often be spotted on breezy, sunny days.

Spend time **watching the birds** in your neighborhood. What do you notice about the way they fly? Do they glide or hover? Are they fast and straight or slow and bouncy? Make notes about what you discover.

 When gazing up at the sky, make sure that you don't look directly at the sun since this can be very dangerous and damage your eyes.

Listening to birdsong can be very calming. What different sounds can you hear?

Shh! We don't want to scare the birds away—try to be as quiet as a mouse.

Stratus clouds are flat in shape and float low in the sky. They can be white or gray.

Stratocumulus clouds are the large, lumpy ones that you see on very cloudy days.

Nimbostratus clouds are dark in color. They provide hours of rain or snowfall.

Cumulonimbus clouds look like cauliflowers and appear before storms.

Pond dipping

You can find many kinds of wonderful wildlife in ponds. Learn how to explore these watery worlds.

dragonfly

1 Fill your jar or tray halfway up with pond water.

2 Place your net slowly and carefully into the pond and move it in a figure eight motion. Bring your net out of the water and turn it inside out into your jar or tray.

Use a magnifying glass to inspect your findings.

Always return the creatures to the same part of the pond.

Pond life

A healthy pond can be home to more than 100 different types of animals. Some live on the surface of the water while others swim below.

pond skater

freshwater shrimp

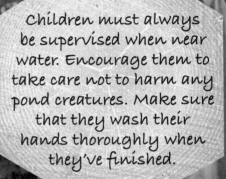

Children must always be supervised when near water. Encourage them to take care not to harm any pond creatures. Make sure that they wash their hands thoroughly when they've finished.

whirligig beetle

froglet

frog

frogspawn

diving beetle

Frog life cycle
A frog is an amphibian. This means it can live in water and on land. An amphibian often starts its life in water, and looks different at each stage of its life.

tadpole

tadpole with legs

pond snail

Terrific trees

You probably pass by trees every day, but do you ever truly pay attention to them? There's so much to learn about these tremendous plants.

Evergreen trees keep their leaves all year round, while deciduous trees drop their leaves in winter.

Try tracking how the trees in your area change over the year.

All trees have an upright trunk.

Nature detective

Try your hand at **bark rubbing**. Place a piece of paper over a tree trunk and rub a crayon on it. The imprint will reveal the pattern of the bark.

Tree shapes

There are so many types of trees that it might seem hard to tell them apart. They might be thin and pointy or wide and stocky. Try to identify their different shapes.

Broad
The branches of a broad tree grow out to the sides.

Palm
Palm trees sprout big leaves at the top of the trunk.

Spreading
These trees have branches that spread out wide.

24

Hello, new friend.
I like your
pointy ears.

Make **forest friends**
by mixing mud with a bit
of water. Splat the mud onto
a tree trunk and press it in.
Then bring your creature to life!
Look for things like fallen leaves
and grass to push into the
mud to create a face.

Forest friends

Round
These trees have
branches that
spread out evenly.

Columnar
A columnar
tree grows
straight up.

Pyramidial
Pointy pyramidial
trees have wide
lower branches.

Weeping
The long branches
of a weeping tree
hang down.

Stuff to do with a stick

A stick can be whatever you want it to be!
What will you transform yours into?

You wil need:

- sticks
- string, yarn, or ribbon
- feathers and fallen leaves or flowers
- safety scissors
- vegetable peeler
- colored pens
- mud
- water

Wild art

What should I turn my stick into?

Wands
Wrap colored string, yarn, or ribbon around a stick then slot in pretty nature finds. Make your wand extra magical by cutting a star shape from a leaf and poking it in.

Mix up some **mud paint** in a pot or dig a little hole in the ground and pour in water. Then, dip your paintbrushes in and start experimenting.

You can do mud painting on paper, the sidewalk, or even on trees!

We love our colorful hats!

⚠️ Show your child how to peel safely and keep a careful eye on them when they try it.

Paintbrushes
Choose leaves, feathers, or flowers to tie onto the ends of sticks. Test them out to see which makes the best paintbrush.

Stick puppets
Use a vegetable peeler to whittle away the end of a stick into a point. Draw on silly faces and hats.

Direct the peeler away from your body.

Wild masterpieces

Artists have always been fascinated by nature. Collect some natural items and think about how they inspire you. Use them to try to create a pattern, like one of the examples here.

You will need:
- collection of natural items found on the ground

Wild art

You might want to add a frame around your creation.

This pattern is symmetrical—it's the same on each side.

Patterns in nature

Nature is full of patterns—from those on tree trunks, leaves, and shells to ripples on the water. Patterns that repeat themselves are called fractals. Try to spot some when you are outside playing.

Spotting **patterns in nature** can be soothing. You might notice your breathing deepen as you relax.

Each branch of a tree copies the shape of the branch that it grew from.

Repeating patterns

When objects are arranged in a repeating order, they make a pattern.

What goes next?

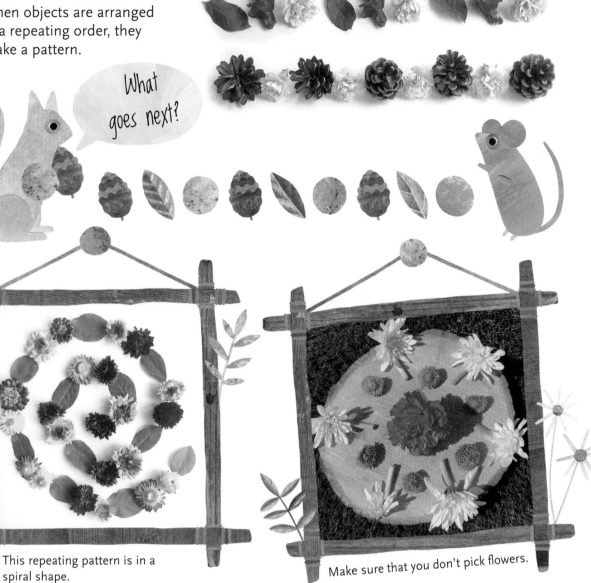

This repeating pattern is in a spiral shape.

Make sure that you don't pick flowers.

These leaves are all the same shape.

A shell is a spiral fractal.

Leaf creatures

You can create so many things from leaves, sticks, and other natural materials. Explore outside and see what you can collect. Then bring the pieces back to life by arranging them into funny creatures.

⚠️ Try to collect a variety of outdoor objects—but watch over your child to make sure they avoid poisonous plants or anything that is still living.

Wild art

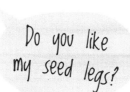
Do you like my seed legs?

Colors and shapes

Choose interesting shapes and colors for the body parts. A curved branch could be the body of a snake, or a piece of green moss might make a cool hairstyle.

What words can you use to describe this leaf?

The natural world is full of color! It will make your creature stand out.

Create faces for us by drawing eyes and a mouth or cut them out of paper.

Spiky leaves or grass are perfect for hair.

Straight twigs work well for legs.

What is your leaf creature called? What's their personality like? Why not make up a fun story about your creation!

Look out for symmetrical leaves for the head.

Can you find a long leaf for the body or legs?

31

Pebble patterns

You will need:
- smooth pebbles
- paint
- paintbrush

Paint your pebbles and turn them into pretty works of art. Place them proudly on display at home, or put them outside for people to find.

Wild art

Painting pebbles

First, give your pebbles a good scrub. Once they're dry, choose bright paint to decorate them. You can transform your pebbles into colorful flowers, bugs, or cover them in patterns... whatever you like!

Choose designs that suit the shapes of each of your pebbles.

Can you make a cozy nest for your pebble creatures?

32

Can I still join the snake, even though I'm a worm?

Count how many stones make up the snake.

Start a **stone snake** where you live or at school. Leave a painted pebble in a safe spot outdoors and encourage others to come along and add their own pebble. How long will the snake grow?

Dominoes

Create your own set of pebble dominoes. Paint a line in the middle of each stone, and up to six dots each side. To play, lay down a pebble. Then the next player lays down a domino that matches one of the ends of the first domino. The player to get rid of all their pebbles first, wins!

Pine cone animals

You will need:
- safety scissors
- felt
- glue
- pine cone

There are many different adorable woodland animals that you can craft using pine cones. Follow these steps to make a felt fox.

1 Cut out the shapes that you need for your fox from felt.

Stick the tail onto the back.

2 Glue the orange triangular shape onto the pine cone, followed by the white shapes. Add the black circles for the eyes and nose. Finally, stick on the tail and feet.

I need some friends! Try creating some more cone creatures.

You can see an owl and a racoon on the next page.

Tiny home

Make a special place for your cone animals to call home.

Ask an adult to help make a table from cut up log pieces.

Welcome to our house.

Cut a piece of bark into the shape of a door, then place it against the base of a tree trunk. Arrange stones into a path that leads up to the door.

Tune into your senses

These games will help you to appreciate the natural world by using all of your senses.

You will need:
- four sticks
- string
- different textured materials like sand and mud
- timer

Nature television

Create a square frame using the same method as on p.10. Ask an adult to tie the frame to two trees, then perform scenes for your friends to watch.

Can we change the channel?

Create a seating area for your audience using logs.

Our senses

We have five senses to help us **explore and understand the world around us**. Your senses all work together to send messages to your brain to let it know what is happening around you.

Our senses are sight, hearing, taste, smell, and touch.

Sensory path

1 Brave a barefoot walk! Choose two or more natural materials that feel different than each other and lay them out on the ground. Don't choose anything too spiky—stick to things such as mud, fallen leaves, soil, and sand.

2 Remove your socks and shoes and close your eyes as you walk across the path. Try to really tune in to how each section feels.

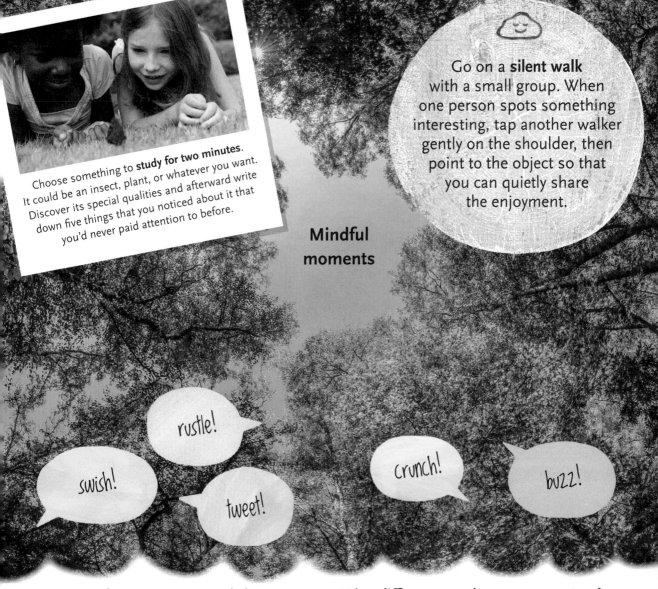

Choose something to **study for two minutes**. It could be an insect, plant, or whatever you want. Discover its special qualities and afterward write down five things that you noticed about it that you'd never paid attention to before.

Go on a **silent walk** with a small group. When one person spots something interesting, tap another walker gently on the shoulder, then point to the object so that you can quietly share the enjoyment.

Mindful moments

swish!

rustle!

tweet!

crunch!

buzz!

Set a timer for two minutes and close your eyes. What **different sounds** can you tune into? When you've finished, note down everything you heard.

Can you guess what you are walking on?

How does it feel?

grass   fallen leaves   a puddle   soil   sand

starting point

Guess the smell

You will need:
- scented natural items
- jars or containers
- scarf or piece of material
- water

How good are you at identifying scents? Put your sense of smell to the test with this fun guessing game.

1 Ask a friend to collect a variety of naturally scented things from outside and place them in different jars.

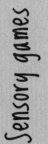

lavender   mint   grass   a fallen flower   soil

2 Use the scarf as a blindfold and ask your friend to remove the lid from one of the jars. Can you guess what's inside just by smelling it?

Try mixing up some fun concoctions by combining several of your scented things in one jar.

You could also pretend to make a magic potion by adding some water into the jar. What spell will you cast?

Try ordering the jars from your favorite to least favorite smell.

Why not use your magic wand from p.26!

Unless you are certain that the items in the jars are not harmful, do not allow your children to taste them.

Something smells good!

Smelling certain plants, like lavender, can have a **calming effect** and promote **restful sleep**.

Say hello to a tree

Get in touch with your senses as you lead a friend on a journey to meet a tree. This is a great game to play with a partner when you're in the woods or at a park.

You will need:
- scarf or piece of material
- partner

Sensory games

2 Carefully guide your friend toward a tree. Ask lots of questions along the way, encouraging them to be aware of their senses and surroundings.

1 Wrap a scarf around your partner's head like a blindfold, or ask them to close their eyes.

What sounds can you hear?

starting point

3 Lead your partner at a slow and steady pace, helping them to avoid obstacles.

How big does the tree seem?

4 Once you've reached the tree, help your partner to explore it.

What does the bark feel like?

Can you wrap your arms around the tree?

Hi there, tree!

5 Guide your partner back to the start. Remove the blindfold or ask them to open their eyes. Can they find their tree again? Then, it's time to swap roles!

Amazing music

Feel like making some music? You don't need to buy expensive equipment to get musical. To make these instruments, all you need are some sticks and a fence—you probably already have everything else!

You will need:
- sticks
- paint
- string
- fence
- recycled things like pots and pans

Stick wind chimes

1 Find an assortment of sticks of varying lengths. Paint them bright colors. Once the sticks have dried, tie them all to one main stick, spacing them out equally, as shown below.

You can also tap the chimes.

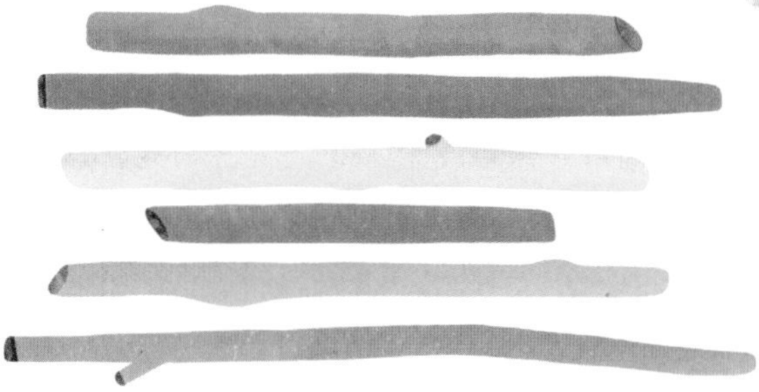

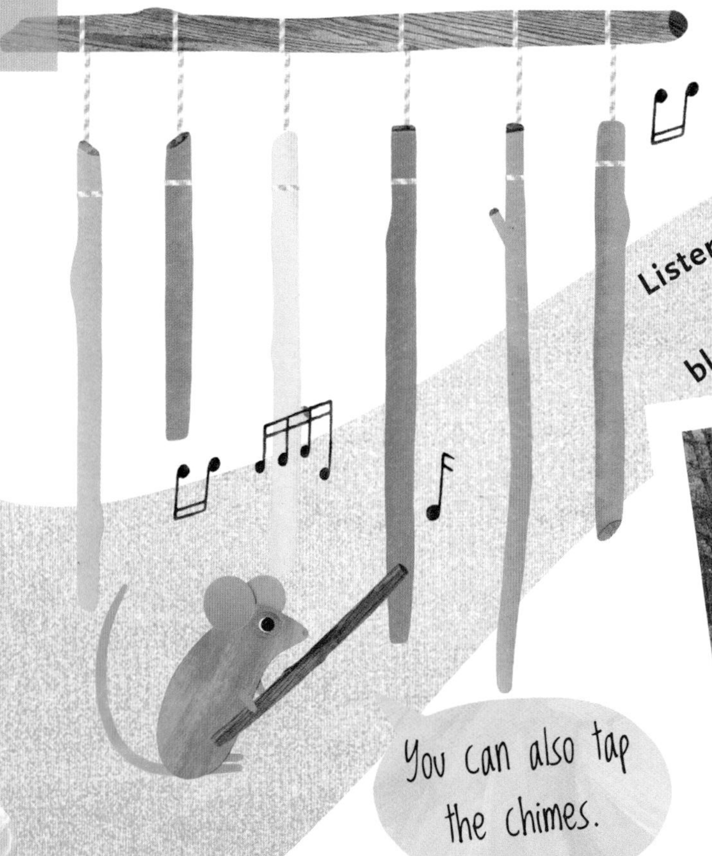

2 Hang your instrument outside, somewhere where the chimes will catch in the breeze.

Listen to the soft sounds as the wind blows the sticks against each other.

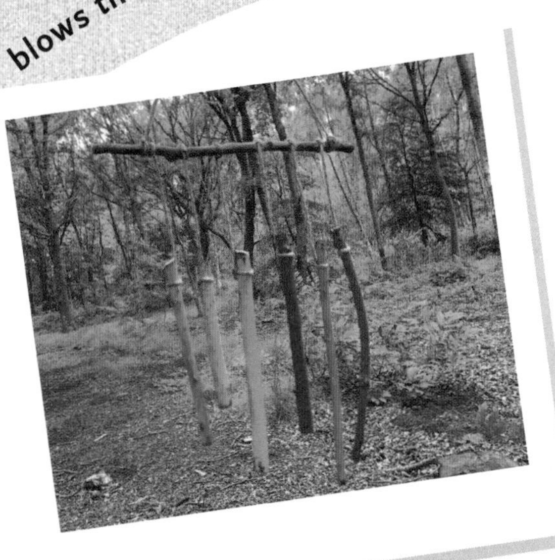

Wooden xylophone

Search for varying lengths of wood that are similar in length but differ in their thickness. Lay them out vertically on top of two horizontal pieces of wood, in size order. Use a stick to hit your xylophone and bang out a tune!

Arrange your sticks by size.

Tap your musical instruments hard and soft, listening to the different effects.

There are many **beautiful sounds in nature**, such as birds singing and water lapping. Music and sound can affect us in different ways. **Listening** to it can calm you down, cheer you up, or even help you concentrate.

Loop string through the fence panels.

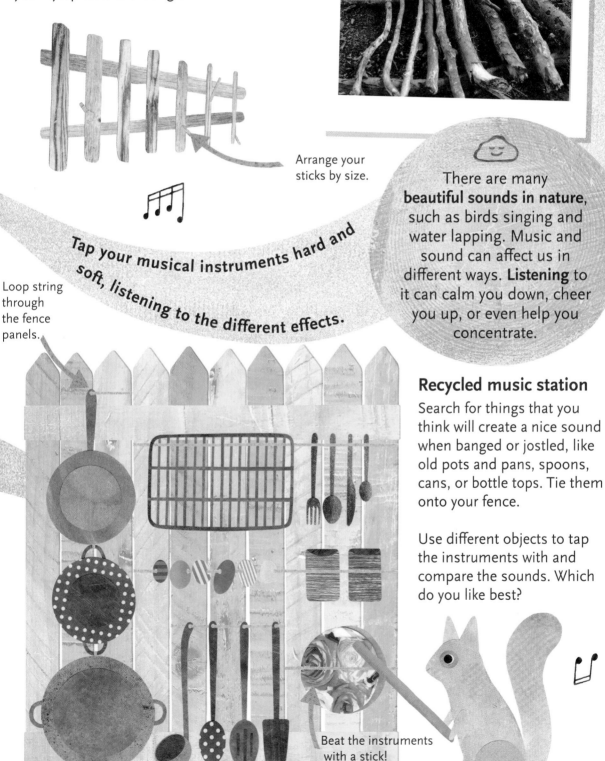

Recycled music station

Search for things that you think will create a nice sound when banged or jostled, like old pots and pans, spoons, cans, or bottle tops. Tie them onto your fence.

Use different objects to tap the instruments with and compare the sounds. Which do you like best?

Beat the instruments with a stick!

43

Beach games

Next time you go to the beach, try out these fun games. They can all be played using things you find or take to the beach.

Sensory games

Three in a row

Draw a grid in the sand as shown below. One player has shells, one has stones. Then take turns placing the items in the squares. The first to get three in a row wins!

Target practice

Draw four circles as shown. Take turns to throw a stone at them, being careful not to throw stones near people. If your stone lands closest to the middle, you win.

Faces in places

Create faces using beach finds, and then position yourself over them to make a shadow person. It's also fun to find pebbles that appear to have faces. How are they feeling?

Your faces might show different feelings. Talk about the emotions.

44

Can I play?

Stacking stones can be relaxing. Find different sized stones, then start with the largest and see how many you can rest on top of each other.

⚠️ Children must be accompanied by an adult when near the ocean.

Use smooth, flat stones.

Fill a bucket race

Cup your hands to hold water and run then backward and forward from the shore to fill up a bucket. Whoever fills it up first, wins!

Glossary

If you're not sure what some of the words in this book mean, use this handy guide to find out.

Amphibian
Animals that can live both in water and on land

Compass
Tool used to find direction

Fractal
Special kind of repeating pattern that can happen in nature

Indigenous Peoples
First people who lived in a place

Life cycle
Stages that a living thing goes through in its life

Magnet
Piece of metal that can attract other magnetic objects to it

Mast
Tall upright post on a boat, that carries a sail

Mindful
Being aware of your thoughts and the world around you

Natural
Existing in nature, not human-made

Navigate
Finding the way through an area

Pattern
Repeated design of shapes and colors

Pebble
Smooth, small stone

Recycle
To use something again or to make it into something new

Raft
Flat floating structure, usually used as a boat

Scent
A distinctive smell

Senses
The five physical senses of touch, smell, taste, hearing, and sight

Sensory
Relating to the five physical senses of touch, smell, taste, hearing, and sight

Shelter
Covered place to hide or stay in for a short time

Weave
Move in and out

Whittle
Carve wood by slicing small pieces from it

Index

Acknowledgments

Meet some of the people who helped to make
The Nature Adventure Book.

Katie, author

Katie was born on a leap year which means she has only had nine birthdays, but has been teaching for fourteen years. She believes that the outdoors is a place for young people to feel inspired, grow, and learn, which is why she became a Forest School leader. She loves to share outdoor activity ideas on Instagram @earlyyearsoutdoor. Katie took lots of the photographs included in this book herself, using her phone. She lives in South Yorkshire, England, with her partner and three children.

Lianne, illustrator

Lianne works from her home studio overlooking the Malvern Hills, England, surrounded by houseplants and accompanied by Captain the cat. She uses paper collage to create illustrations from her collection of colorful, painted, and patterned papers. She loves wildlife, walking in nature, and collects lots of nature books for inspiration.

We hope you enjoy reading this book as much as we enjoyed making it.

We helped too!

DK would like to thank: Clare Lloyd for proofreading and Helen Peters for the index.

Picture credits

The publisher would like to thank the following for their kind permission to reproduce their photographs:

(Key: a-above; b-below/bottom; c-center; f-far; l-left; r-right; t-top)

4 **123RF.com:** denyskuvaiev (bc). **Dreamstime.com:** Sam74100 (clb). 9 **Alamy Stock Photo:** Paul Hawkett (t). 14 **Dreamstime.com:** Robert Kneschke (cra). 17 **Dreamstime.com:** Roman Milert. 18 **123RF.com:** lightfieldstudios (br). **Getty Images:** Bongarts / Alexandra Beier (cl). 24 **Getty Images:** Universal Images Group / Marka (clb). 28 **Dreamstime.com:** Vladimir Loschi (bc). 29 **123RF.com:** Petra Schüller / pixelelfe (br). **Dreamstime.com:** Euphotica (bl). 37 **Getty Images:** Cultura / Tim Hall (tl); Moment / paul mansfield photography (t). 41 **Getty Images:** Cultura / Janie Airey (cb)
Cover images: Back: Getty Images: Cultura / Janie Airey (tl)

All other images © Dorling Kindersley
For further information see: www.dkimages.com